SILENT SKY

Lauren Gunderson

BROADWAY
BOOK CLUB

NOTE ON BILLING

SPECIAL NOTE ON SONGS/RECORDINGS

SILENT SKY was commissioned by and premiered at South Coast Repertory (Marc Masterson, Artistic Director; Paula Tomei, Managing Director), in Costa Mesa, California, with support from the Elizabeth George Foundation, as part of the 2011 Pacific Playwrights Festival. It was directed by Anne Justine D'Zmura; the scenic design was by John Iacovelli; the costume design was by David Kay Mickelsen; the lighting design was by York Kennedy; the original music was by Lewis Flinn; the projection design was by John Crawford; the dramaturg was John Glore; and the production manager was Joshua Marchesi. The cast was as follows:

HENRIETTA LEAVITT .... Monette Magrath
MARGARET LEAVITT .... Erin Cottrell
PETER SHAW .... Nick Toren
ANNIE CANNON .... Colette Kilroy
WILLIAMINA FLEMING .... Amelia White

CHARACTERS

HENRIETTA LEAVITT (LEH-vit): 30s, brilliant, meticulous, excited — almost always wearing a period hearing-aid.

MARGARET LEAVITT: 30s, homebody, creative, sweet, sister.

PETER SHAW: 30s, the head astronomer's apprentice ... and the man.

ANNIE CANNON: 40s, the leader, terse and sure, grows into a firebrand.

WILLIAMINA FLEMING: 50s, smart as a whip and fun, Scottish.

SETTINGS

1900–1920.
Star field.
The Harvard Observatory 2nd-floor offices.
Leavitt home, Wisconsin.
Ocean liner on the Atlantic.
Henrietta's home, Cambridge, MA.

NOTES

Sets: Simple, representational, flexible — e.g. a period desk, not a whole room. Swift transitions are key.

Stars: The star field from the Northern Hemisphere should be almost ever-present; even if the stage lights disappear, the stars shine and cradle the set.

Photographic Plates: These should be black and white window-pane-sized glass of the star field. They are negatives of the true night sky — stars are black and sky is white. For examples see: http://tdc-www.harvard.edu/plates/gallery/

Music: Margaret's piano composition and playing should be live (seemingly), then augmented by a fully encompassing sound as the stars take over. *(See Note on Music on following page.)*

Magellanic: MAJ-eh-LAN-ic
Cepheid: SEH-fid
Andromedae: An-DRAH-muh-DIE

More research and images here: SilentSkyPlay.tumblr.com

NOTE ON MUSIC

Original music composed for the play by Jenny Giering is available for licensing through the Play Service. Please visit the SILENT SKY page on www.dramatists.com for more information regarding the ordering and use of the original music, and to hear samples.

"In our troubled days it is good to have something outside our planet, something fine and distant for comfort."

—Annie Jump Cannon

SILENT SKY

ACT ONE

Scene 1

The late evening sky outside Henrietta and Margaret's father's rural Wisconsin church — about 1900 ...

A ruddy sun sets on Henrietta — a fiercely smart woman, curious, energetic, spilling over her own traditionalism. Dressed primly and warmly, she points to the sky above her.

HENRIETTA. Heaven's up there, they say. "Pearly clouds, pearly gates," they say. They don't know much about astronomy, I say. *(The sun is gone and the sky darkens into night.)* The science of light on high. Of all that is far-off and lonely and stuck in the deepest dark of space. Dark but for billions and billions of ... *(The first star to peek out. A single note accompanies it.)* Exceptions. *(As the sister stars emerge. Another note.)* And I insist on the exceptional. *(As the night sky suddenly brightens into stark day — Margaret sneaks up on Henrietta and pinches her.)* Ow — What are you doing?
MARGARET. You know church is about to start. You know this and you're avoiding it and you've been caught.
HENRIETTA. I haven't been caught, I've been attacked.
MARGARET. With love.
HENRIETTA. With pinches. What kind of world is this.
MARGARET. You're not wearing your hearing-aid, you're fair game. Church. Now.
HENRIETTA. I can't right now.
MARGARET. Oh yes you can, We'reWaitingI'mfreezingComeIn.

HENRIETTA. Margie, I'm sorry but I cannot sit still right now.

MARGARET. The only thing you have to do in church is sit still. Now tell me what's going on or come inside.

HENRIETTA. I've been trying to tell you all week but you're busy and you're barking and —

MARGARET. *(Bark-like.) I don't bark.* I'm running the house, and Daddy's running the church, and *you* — What are you doing? Staying up all night? In the cold? Like a moth?

HENRIETTA. What is wrong with you this morning, Miss Jumpy.

MARGARET. I'm not jumpy —

HENRIETTA. I'm not a moth —

MARGARET. Why are we still outside?!

HENRIETTA. *Because.* They have a job for me at Harvard. At the Observatory. Actual astronomy.

MARGARET. Since when were you even looking for a job.

HENRIETTA. Since they offered. Margie, this is an extraordinary thing. They need mathematicians and they asked me specifically —

MARGARET. Harvard asked *you*?

HENRIETTA. Yes and please don't hold back your tone of shock.

MARGARET. This is shocking — I am shocked.

HENRIETTA. And I'm ... leaving. I'm taking the job and I'm leaving. *(Holding out a letter. Beat.)*

MARGARET. You've always been leaving.

HENRIETTA. Next week.

MARGARET. Next...? Oh Henri. Now wait. We need to discuss this as a family.

HENRIETTA. Margie, this could be my best life and it's right in front of me.

MARGARET. And I'm still freezing. *(Turns to go.)*

HENRIETTA. Margie, talk to me —

MARGARET. Fine — yes — I know that we were never going to be grow-old-next-to-each-other kind of sisters, and the way you drive me crazy makes that for the best — but — Henrietta this is extreme.

HENRIETTA. Exactly. Come with me. *(Small pause.)*

MARGARET. Oh, Henri, please.

HENRIETTA. Both of us. Come on.

MARGARET. What are you talking about? That's absurd.

HENRIETTA. Only a little! You're the only person who understands me, and you're always up for an adventure, and I *do* want to get old and scrappy with you.

MARGARET. I did not say scrappy.

HENRIETTA. You should come with me and fire up your heart!

MARGARET. What are you talking about?

HENRIETTA. The edge of the wide world!

MARGARET. It's Boston.

HENRIETTA. A blaze of learning!

MARGARET. A *blaze*?

HENRIETTA. A blaze! And Radcliffe is nearby and they have a music school.

MARGARET. Henri. Slow down.

HENRIETTA. You don't have to stay here. You can be happy, you can loose yourself —

MARGARET. *Loose* my — ? No. Stop. Do not start wearing bloomers.

HENRIETTA. Margie.

MARGARET. *Wait.* There are women these days, and they wear pants, and it's ridiculous. Now I have to play the hymns for the service that started ten minutes ago, and thank you, sister, my fingers are numb.

HENRIETTA. *I need you to convince Daddy to give me my dowry. (This stops Margie cold.)* I'm serious. Very. Please talk to him.

MARGARET. *Why do I get all the yelling jobs?*

HENRIETTA. You're so good at it.

MARGARET. This is your future, Henrietta. You know for certain that you'll never marry, you'll never fall in love — people do that. Uncoordinated, unplanned emotion — Just the word "spinster," Henrietta, please.

HENRIETTA. I need to start my life ... with Daddy's money.

MARGARET. Next the bloomers. Whiskey with suffragettes.

HENRIETTA. I'm not a cowboy.

MARGARET. You know what I'm talking about.

HENRIETTA. I'm talking about astronomy. You keep talking about terrible pants.

MARGARET. *It starts with pants.* It's a changing world. And some things should be sacred. And I'm not saying you shouldn't go — but I worry. It's far away, that place, and it's crowded, and you're still here in my sight and I worry.

HENRIETTA. I'll be doing math. Don't worry.

MARGARET. Why not stay here and live with us and ... teach?

HENRIETTA. No.

MARGARET. Like every other girl with your temperament.

HENRIETTA. *I like my temperament* and I don't want it stuffed in a schoolhouse. I have questions, I have fundamental problems with the state of human knowledge! Who are we, why are we — where are we?!

MARGARET. Wisconsin.

HENRIETTA. In the universe!

MARGARET. Still Wisconsin.

HENRIETTA. *Margie*, I am not just curious I am charged and poised and you *know* that I'll just get more and more annoying until I go — You know this — You know this. *(Margie knows this. Pause.)*

MARGARET. One day there will be a word for you. Just — for me, for our father, who will only after much snorting approve of this — when you go? Take a Bible.

HENRIETTA. I think Harvard has those.

MARGARET. You know what I mean. We look in the same direction — *(Points up.)* but our understanding is … distinct.

HENRIETTA. I love you. It's too cold for God.

MARGARET. That's why we keep Him inside.

HENRIETTA. Margie, come with me.

MARGARET. *I can't.*

HENRIETTA. Why not?

MARGARET. Because Father counts on me, and if you leave I can't leave, and I don't want to leave and … Samuel proposed. *(Moment.)*

HENRIETTA. What.

MARGARET. To marry.

HENRIETTA. Who?

MARGARET. Henri.

HENRIETTA. I mean, "when."

MARGARET. This morning, thank you for noticing.

HENRIETTA. Aha, jumpy.

MARGARET. Yes. Other people's lives are also in progress.

HENRIETTA. Is he…?

MARGARET. Inside looking very attentive until the service ends. And I answer.

HENRIETTA. What's your answer?

MARGARET. Of course I will.

HENRIETTA. To Samuel?

MARGARET. Well I wanted to talk to you first.

HENRIETTA. You'd leave me for Samuel?

MARGARET. You just said you're leaving me!

HENRIETTA. Not for Samuel!

MARGARET. He is very good and … *(Small pause.)*

HENRIETTA. Yes. He is.

MARGARET. He is. And I'm happy.

HENRIETTA. Then … I am too. *(They hug — marriage! Yay!)* Come with me.

MARGARET. Just … come back. *(Squeezes Henri's hand and runs inside.)*

HENRIETTA. And so. I go. *(Preps herself as … The Harvard Observatory falls into place around her … We hear Margaret singing "For the Beauty of the Earth.")*

MARGARET.

For the beauty of the Earth,
For the glory of the skies;
For the love which from our birth,
Over and around us lies;

Lord of all, to Thee we raise
This, our hymn of grateful praise.
(Margaret fades away. Transition …)

Scene 2

Henrietta stands in the vacant room of the Harvard Observatory — A small wooden room like an attic — desks, file drawers, and boxes fill the room.

Peter — unintentionally handsome, a bit bumbling — enters briskly, a pencil behind his ear, charts, papers.

HENRIETTA. Excuse me, is this the Observatory office?

PETER. Oh — yes — Hello. You must be my ten o'clock. Miss Leavitt. You are Miss Leavitt?

HENRIETTA. I am. Henrietta Leavitt and I'm thrilled to —

PETER. Good. We'll make this quick. It's not that complicated.

HENRIETTA. May I just say how pleased I am to meet you, Dr. Pickering. I am so honored —

PETER. No.

13

HENRIETTA. I'm not?

PETER. *I'm* not.

HENRIETTA. You're not Dr. Pickering?

PETER. I am.

HENRIETTA. You *are* Dr. Pickering?

PETER. So sorry. My name is Peter Shaw. I work for Pickering.

HENRIETTA. Oh. Lovely. Mr. Shaw. Nice to meet you. Colleagues then. *(Peter snorts.)*

PETER. You actually work *for* me. And I work for him. So.

HENRIETTA. So we're still colleagues it would seem.

PETER. Technically yes but —

HENRIETTA. And here I thought Harvard was such a technical place.

PETER. No, I just mean that — I mean of course it is it's just — You see I'm Dr. Pickering's apprentice — Junior Fellow in Astronomical Research, summa cum laude, Mathematics *and* Physics.

HENRIETTA. And if you spot me I'll swoon.

PETER. What?

HENRIETTA. It's a technical term. Now, Mr. Shaw I've come a long way and I'm quite anxious to get started. *(He's staring a bit too long at her.)* May I?

PETER. Hm?

HENRIETTA. Get started. Or just point me to the telescope and I'll be fine.

PETER. The telescope?

HENRIETTA. *(Looking out a window.)* Is that it? The Great Refractor.

PETER. Yes, but —

HENRIETTA. One of the largest in the world.

PETER. I am very aware. Quite a point of pride for us. But. *This* is the workroom for you girls ... to work. In here.

HENRIETTA. A short orientation then.

PETER. We bring the Girls' Department photographic plates from the telescope — latest technology.

HENRIETTA. Yes. Good. Question. Why all women?

PETER. Oh. This is great. Pickering got fed up with the boys he was sent and said — really said this — that his housekeeper could do better, so he hired her. And she did better. Now it's quite a women's ... world ... up here.

HENRIETTA. I was expecting the usual world.

PETER. Oh I make regular rounds.

HENRIETTA. Rounds?

PETER. I come around.

HENRIETTA. To what end?

PETER. *(Snort-laughs.)* Evaluation. Of course.

HENRIETTA. Mr. Shaw, I also graduated summa cum laude, from Radcliffe, which is basically Harvard in skirts and lucky for us the universe doesn't much care what you wear, so my expertise and yours might just complement each other's if we can get past this encroachingly unpleasant first impression. *(Re: her hearing-aid.)* Or I could take this out, and you could keep … orienting.

PETER. Well. You'll fit right in the harem.

HENRIETTA. The WHAT?

PETER. Oh — no — nono — it's just a name — a joke — "Pickering's harem." It's a compliment.

HENRIETTA. If you're a concubine.

PETER. He picks the best is what we mean. We could just call you that — "Pickering's Best." "Pickering's Picks" — That's got a ring. *(Glances quickly at her hand —)* You don't. *(Henrietta looks too, hides her hand. Pause. Awkward.)*

HENRIETTA. I was supposed to meet Dr. Pickering at ten.

PETER. Yes. Yes. And he sends his warmest welcome through me. He was detained. More important — not "important," *pressing.* More pressing matters. I'll show you around.

HENRIETTA. I'll come back.

PETER. There's no need for that.

HENRIETTA. I'd prefer to speak directly to the Head of the Department.

PETER. Miss Leavitt —

HENRIETTA. Mr. Shaw. I don't mean to be brisk — maybe a little if that would drive home the point that I'm *finally* here. After a long time not being anywhere. And I'd really like to get started, and all you've thus far conveyed is that I'm in some kind of *math harem* waiting to be *picked* — and that doesn't sound right at *all.*

PETER. I am so sorry. And Dr. Pickering is thrilled to have you here. And I'd get in a lot of trouble with him if I ran you off on your first day. So. Please stay. We'd very much like you to stay. *(Pause.)*

HENRIETTA. You don't sound very excited about all this work.

PETER. Well, it is *work.*

HENRIETTA. It's not your — how best to make you uncomfortable — *passion*?

PETER. That's a bit excessive for physics.

15

HENRIETTA. Is it? I find the very notion of this work to be a thrill — a bracing excitement. And it's just something you *do*?

PETER. Well I enjoy the work, of course I do. It's interesting and reasoned and sound and my father pulled a lot of strings to — WhyDidYouSay"Passion"?

HENRIETTA. Unlike for some people, following this curiosity was not easy. I had to insist, which requires a dedicated desire unmatched by reason, which is called passion. You should try it. *(Tiny pause.)*

PETER. *(Blurting this out.)* I sing. Gilbert and Sullivan — I wanted to be an actor — Dad thought not — But — I still sing — On occasion — With enthusiasm. Does that count?

HENRIETTA. Technically. *(Slightly embarrassed, he picks up a glass star plate. Back to orienting.)*

PETER. Well. Here you go. One of the plates you'll be working with. A slice of heaven.

HENRIETTA. Beautiful. I should take one to my father.

PETER. *Excuse me.*

HENRIETTA. He's a pastor.

PETER. These never leave the premises.

HENRIETTA. You said "heaven," I was joking.

PETER. Harvard property —

HENRIETTA. Of course —

PETER. Very expensive —

HENRIETTA. And if you don't mention the attempted larceny and I won't mention the musicals. *(She extends her hand, he takes it, shakes it.)*

PETER. You're … curious.

HENRIETTA. In every way. *(A bustle outside — women coming back from break.)*

PETER. Oh, they're back. Watch out for Miss Fleming — Scottish stock. Swift and angry.

HENRIETTA. Oh my.

PETER. And Miss Cannon — don't get in her way, her name is Dickensian.

HENRIETTA. But I'd like to ask about —

PETER. What else can I tell you — Penmanship — key. Delicacy with the plates, they crack.

HENRIETTA. Mr. Shaw —

PETER. Twenty-five cents an hour.

HENRIETTA. I would love a chance to pursue —

PETER. It's good money for women's work.

HENRIETTA. It's volunteering.

PETER. What are you asking, Miss Leavitt? *(Annie and Williamina enter, unnoticed.)*

HENRIETTA. That I might more fully engage in the ideas here?

PETER. Other than doing the work you've been hired to do?

HENRIETTA. Other than, pardon me, *do your math.* Now when may I use the telescope?

PETER. *(Flustered, not dismissive.)* Well. You can't. *(Henrietta is too shocked to answer. Annie clears her throat.)*

ANNIE. I'll take over, Mr. Shaw.

PETER. Yes — very good — Started to brief her.

WILLIAMINA. Then I'd be brief.

PETER. Yes — well — Good day, ladies. *(To Henrietta.)* I'll see you ... around. *(He leaves. They look at Henrietta.)*

WILLIAMINA. Welcome, Miss Leavitt.

HENRIETTA. Thank you. Hello. I was so excited to be here that I fear I might've scared him.

WILLIAMINA. Easy to do. Williamina Fleming. I like you.

HENRIETTA. Thank you.

ANNIE. Annie Cannon. I haven't decided.

HENRIETTA. Oh. Miss Cannon. I know that I probably shouldn't have gone on like that with him.

ANNIE. No you shouldn't.

HENRIETTA. And I'm sorry if I made a poor impression —

ANNIE. Harvard Observatory is the pinnacle of the astronomical community. The academic world looks to us.

HENRIETTA. To "bookkeep the stars," if you talk to Mr. Shaw.

ANNIE. Which is why we try not to talk to Mr. Shaw. We are mapping the sky, Miss Leavitt. If doing what has never been done before sounds unimportant to you, uninspired? I'd leave before you are asked to. Otherwise, show some respect.

HENRIETTA. Of course. And I would never —

ANNIE. Respect is a *quiet* thing, Miss Leavitt. Practice this.

HENRIETTA. Yes, Miss Cannon.

ANNIE. Practice now. *(Henrietta nods. Pause. Will holds up one of the photographic star plates.)*

WILLIAMINA. Let me show you what we do here, Miss Leavitt. This is the latest technology. A photograph of the stars. And we chart every point of light on every one.

ANNIE. Every single one.

WILLIAMINA. Every scattered sneeze of them.

ANNIE. *Will*, don't be crude

WILLIAMINA. They look like ground pepper till you get the hang of it.

ANNIE. Williamina is our best photometer, from whom you'll learn much if she doesn't get herself fired. *(Williamina smiles, Annie glares.)*

WILLIAMINA. I used to be her boss.

ANNIE. You still *are*. We share leadership of this department —

WILLIAMINA. She outdid me with those letters.

ANNIE. I did no such thing —

WILLIAMINA. The star classifications were her idea.

ANNIE. A *collective* effort, I assure you.

HENRIETTA. Star classifications? That's your work?

WILLIAMINA. Oh yes indeed, the sky was a riot until Miss Cannon coded it. *I* wanted to give every star a number based on color — but *she* insisted on labeling stars with *letters* based on *temperature* —

ANNIE. Ladies —

WILLIAMINA.	HENRIETTA.
OBAFGKM.	OBAFGKM —
Yes.	

HENRIETTA. You created a ... standard, Miss Cannon. My goodness. I'm so honored. I'm sure you'd laugh, but my professors made us memorize your letters using this ridiculous phrase —

WILLIAMINA. She also made up that ridiculous phrase.

ANNIE. But I didn't mean for it to find its way into textbooks.

HENRIETTA. "Oh Be A Fine Girl, Kiss Me." You did that too?

WILLIAMINA. She had a muse.

ANNIE. *Miss Fleming.*

WILLIAMINA. She thought it would be best for the boys. That's all they think about anyway.

ANNIE. Let's get back to work please.

WILLIAMINA. *(To Henrietta — whispering.)* Because she's the boss.

ANNIE. *I wouldn't have to be if you'd take this seriously, which is a ridiculous request of a woman who started the department. (To Henrietta.)* You know Will was the first woman to ever hold the title "curator" in astronomy? And the Draper Catalogue is *all* her work — She discovered stars, and nebulae, novae — She's the reason that I'm here, and even if she has far too much fun I am the first to admit that she is fundamental to this institution.

WILLIAMINA. *(To Henrietta.)* And that, new friend, is how you introduce yourself without boasting.

ANNIE. I quit.

WILLIAMINA. *(To Annie.)* "Oh Be A Fine Grandma."

HENRIETTA. It's a great phrase.

ANNIE. We have WORK. TO DO. And Dr. Pickering is a very particular man.

WILLIAMINA. He calls us his *harem*.

ANNIE. He's joking.

WILLIAMINA. He's not. He measures a project in "girl hours."

ANNIE. He's joking.

WILLIAMINA. He's not. Sometimes "kilo-girl hours."

ANNIE. The point is, we're busy because we're essential.

WILLIAMINA. We're the dirt. *(Annie glares. Correcting ...)* From which mighty oaks grow.

HENRIETTA. And do we have a title of some sort?

WILLIAMINA. We do indeed. Congratulations, Miss Leavitt, you are now a computer.

HENRIETTA. What's a computer?

ANNIE. One who computes.

WILLIAMINA. Notate the plates, transfer the data, input the data, process, record, next star.

HENRIETTA. And the plates. How do I read them?

WILLIAMINA. Star Spanking. *(Annie reveals a wire-and-glass paddle like a small fly-swatter. Annie places the spanker over the plate.)*

ANNIE. Align the spanker with a star. The matching dot indicates how bright that star is. Record magnitude, position, date, and repeat until you fill up the logbook.

WILLIAMINA. Or go slightly crazy.

HENRIETTA. And what about working on our own ideas? Using the telescope for our own work?

ANNIE. You don't.

HENRIETTA. Oh. But I thought this was — ?

ANNIE. We collect, report, and maintain the largest stellar archive in the world. And we resist the temptation to analyze it.

HENRIETTA. But you just said how much you discovered here — both of you.

WILLIAMINA. Resisting doesn't always work.

ANNIE. Can you do this job, Miss Leavitt?

HENRIETTA. Of course I can.

ANNIE. I need the consistent, not the creative.

WILLIAMINA. She can do it, Annie. She understands.

ANNIE. Good. Please show Miss Leavitt to her station.

WILLIAMINA. Will do, Mr. President.

ANNIE. You make me crazy and you know you make me crazy.

WILLIAMINA. Balance of power, darling. *(Annie exits.)* Alright, you. More questions?

HENRIETTA. Is she mean or just to me?

WILLIAMINA. Oh nono. She's just meticulous. And blunt. And she sings.

HENRIETTA. Sings what?

WILLIAMINA. Like a crow, but still. Shows her humanity — atonal though it may be. You want her on your side. She's always on the right one.

HENRIETTA. Good. Because I have some pressing issues with … science.

WILLIAMINA. The whole of it?

HENRIETTA. A lot of it. As far as I can tell we do not appear to know where we are. Astronomically. Which is shocking. This is the modern age. We've been looking *up* for millennia and we don't know how far away those stars are? We don't know if the Milky Way is the universe? That's just unacceptable.

WILLIAMINA. You're fun. But here's some perspective. I was Pickering's housekeeper before he brought me here. So we're a lot of things, but at present we are cleaning up the universe for the men. And making fun of them behind their backs. It's worked for centuries. *(Annie enters with more plates.)*

ANNIE. Working isn't talking.

| Here we like to say: | WILLIAMINA. |
| The sky's the limit. | The sky's the limit. |

WILLIAMINA. And there's so damn much of it.

ANNIE. And so we work. *(She deposits the plates. The women sit down at their desks and work. As they label each star — a single bright star pops into being in their spare sky, accompanied by a musical note. Rote.)* Star Name —

HENRIETTA. Star Name —

WILLIAMINA. Star Name —

HENRIETTA. Alpha Leonis 3982.

ANNIE. Beta Orionis 1713.

WILLIAMINA. Ninety-five degrees declination.

ANNIE. Seventy-three degrees —

HENRIETTA. Fifty degrees.

WILLIAMINA. Spectral Class B.

ANNIE. Spectral Class B. *(Henrietta takes out her hearing device — The sound of the room softens, dulls. Henrietta and Margaret are normal volume.)*

WILLIAMINA. Magnitude: one-point-two-five.

ANNIE. Magnitude: point-six-five. *(Margaret appears in a letter.)*

MARGARET. Henrietta! We miss you.

HENRIETTA. Star Name —

MARGARET. And I can't stand the conversation since you left.

HENRIETTA. Alpha Andromedae 15.

MARGARET. Everyone is so sensible.

HENRIETTA. Eighty degrees declination.

MARGARET. Please write back.

HENRIETTA. Uh-huh. Thirty-three right ascension. *(Peter enters.)*

PETER. Morning, ladies.

WILLIAMINA. Correct on both counts, Mr. Shaw.

ANNIE. Good morning, Mr. Shaw. Back again?

WILLIAMINA. And so soon.

PETER. Just passing by — Dropping these off — Picking these up.

HENRIETTA. Spectral Class A.

PETER. Hello, Miss Leavitt.

HENRIETTA. Magnitude: two-point — What? Oh. Hello, Mr. Shaw. How are you today?

PETER. Good … *(Lovely, awkward pause, during which he finds nothing else to say, except.)* Bye. *(He leaves quickly, embarrassed again.)*

HENRIETTA. He's an odd one.

WILLIAMINA. And getting odder.

ANNIE. Star Name —

HENRIETTA. Star Name —

WILLIAMINA. Star Name — *(Time is passing as the sky fills up in swatches. Another letter.)*

MARGARET. Henri! Wish you'd be here for Thanksgiving. Daddy's planning a marvelous sermon on *family*.

HENRIETTA. Uh-huh. Magnitude: two-point-eight.

MARGARET. You missed the news …

HENRIETTA. Star Name.

MARGARET. I'm pregnant!

HENRIETTA. *(Finally stopping.)* Oh Margie. Oh my goodness.

21

MARGARET. I think Daddy is happier that I am. And think of it, you're going to be an aunt.

HENRIETTA. I'm going to be an aunt. And you. A mother? Congratulations, Margie, that's such — *(Annie coughs at Henrietta. Henrietta hides the letter.)* Star Name: Alpha Cygnus. Spectral Class A. *(Time is passing as the sky fills up in swatches. Peter enters again …)*

PETER. Hellohello. Here I come. Coming around.

WILLIAMINA. A lot nowadays.

HENRIETTA. *(Putting in her hearing-aid.)* What's going on?

PETER. Just want to make sure she's — everyone's oriented.

WILLIAMINA. It's been half a year now. I think she can find the bathroom.

HENRIETTA. Am I doing something wrong, Mr. Shaw?

PETER. Nono. Of course not. I'm just … curious.

WILLIAMINA. Uh-huh.

PETER. About the … data.

WILLIAMINA. *(To Annie.)* Oh yes, he's dreaming about the "data."

ANNIE. We're a bit busy today, Mr. Shaw. Unless you have a message for the room?

PETER. Oh — yes — Dr. Pickering and I wanted Miss Leavitt's opinion on something of great interest. If I may steal a moment.

ANNIE. You may borrow Miss Leavitt, not steal her.

PETER. Of course. Just an expression.

WILLIAMINA. Was it?

HENRIETTA. I'm so glad Dr. Pickering values my opinion. I didn't know he noticed me at all.

PETER. He did. And does. *(He holds a star plate and points to a spot, but this is obviously just a reason to get close to her.)* I was — We were wondering if you could explain what sort of phenomena this might be? I haven't seen anything like it on the other plates and thought of you — *that you* might offer some clarity. *(She looks. She knows.)*

HENRIETTA. Well, Mr. Shaw. That's definitely a scratch.

PETER. Is it?

HENRIETTA. I'm guessing someone's pocketwatch or perhaps a belt buckle?

PETER. A scratch.

WILLIAMINA. We can name it after you if you'd like?

PETER. No need. Glad that's cleared up. Time to go.

ANNIE. Yes indeed.

HENRIETTA. *(Something in her warms to him.)* Thank you. For asking, Mr. Shaw. We're always here if you need us. *(Peter deeply appreciates Henrietta in this moment. He smiles and leaves just as —
Time is passing as the sky fills up in swatches. Another letter.)*
MARGARET. Henrietta.
ANNIE. Thirty-two degrees.
MARGARET. Will we see you for Easter?
WILLIAMINA. Magnitude: six-point-two.
MARGARET. Daddy's asking for you,
HENRIETTA. Spectral Class B.
MARGARET. And I'd love to have you home —
HENRIETTA. Forty-five —
MARGARET. Henrietta, it's —
HENRIETTA. Magnitude —
MARGARET. *Henrietta.*
HENRIETTA. What? Yes. What?
MARGARET. I have a son.
HENRIETTA. Oh. Oh, Margie.
MARGARET. His name is Michael.
HENRIETTA. You have a son.
MARGARET. You should meet him.
HENRIETTA. I should — I *will* — How did this happen already?
MARGARET. It's April.
HENRIETTA. Oh my. Is it? It is.
MARGARET. Henrietta, let me tell you, babies are remarkable.
HENRIETTA. I'm sure but I'm sorry — I'm just so busy.
MARGARET. Too busy for me?
HENRIETTA. Too busy for *me* at the moment.
MARGARET. Can't you come home?
HENRIETTA. There are a lot of stars out there.
MARGARET. But you'd be so proud. I've found my calling!
HENRIETTA. Uh-huh.
MARGARET. I will compose!
HENRIETTA. Music? How nice.
MARGARET. When the baby's down and everything's clean it's just me and the piano.
HENRIETTA. That's great.
MARGARET. It's not a hobby.
HENRIETTA. I have to work.
MARGARET. It's very exciting.

HENRIETTA. It is. And I'm sorry I can't come home and I'm sure I'm letting you down, but I've got this work, and you've got yours, and I can't play house with you right now.

MARGARET. I don't like this mood.

HENRIETTA. I promise I'll come home.

MARGARET. *You won't.* You're hardening in some urban office and it's making you flinty.

HENRIETTA. Margie, stop.

MARGARET. I know that there's more to life than that.

HENRIETTA. Than nature?

MARGARET. Than math. There's more out there —

HENRIETTA. *Then why do you stay so close to home?* Why do you excel at every ordinary thing and then chastise *me* about what else is "out there." I specialize in what's "out there" — and let me tell you that "out there" does not happen *on a farm. (Beat.)*

MARGARET. *(Cold to her.)* Check the post. Father sent a book.

HENRIETTA. Oh no. A Bible?

MARGARET. If it were a Bible I would've said "Bible" — It's a book.

HENRIETTA. On what?

ANNIE. Miss Leavitt?

MARGARET. I don't know, Henrietta. I've got this life, you've got yours. *(Margaret vanishes. Peter reenters, approaches Henrietta — total, sweetheart nervous.)*

PETER. Round and round we go.

ANNIE. Mr. Shaw.

PETER. Ladies of the Logbook.

ANNIE. By God you'd better have a supernova on those plates.

WILLIAMINA. *(To Henrietta softly.)* You know he's here for you.

HENRIETTA. *(To Will.) What.*

PETER. Nothing that exciting. I was just hoping to speak to Miss Leavitt.

HENRIETTA. *(To Will.)* Mr. Shaw?

PETER. The work she's — *you're all* doing is just — well I find it *bracing.*

ANNIE. And I find it hard to work with such interruptions, if you don't mind —

PETER. *(To Annie.)* I'm sorry, I can come back later —

ANNIE.	WILLIAMINA.
NO.	NO.

PETER. On my rounds.

ANNIE. *(Exploding.)* MR. SHAW. There is an inverse relationship between time lost on your rounds and the life of my overqualified staff, any one of whom you may speak to *after* work, so come in or stay out but you *must have reason to be here or cease. Coming. Around.* *(Pause. Peter looks to Henrietta, then back to Annie.)*

PETER. *(Breath, cheerily.)* See you tomorrow. *(Smiles at Henrietta, then leaves.)*

ANNIE. Sweet boy — I'm going to shoot him.

WILLIAMINA. *(To Henrietta.)* You see what I mean about him. He never thought we were "bracing" before.

HENRIETTA. Can we talk about *anything* else, please. Miss Cannon, help.

WILLIAMINA. Just so we're all clear: *He fancies you.*

HENRIETTA. I don't care. I barely know him. I *don't* know him. We just — we work. He comes around.

WILLIAMINA. Like a hungry cat.

HENRIETTA. Who's the cat? Am I the cat?

ANNIE. *You're* not the cat.

HENRIETTA. I better not be. I mean, my goodness, I wouldn't even know where to begin.

WILLIAMINA. He'd be happy to help you with that.

ANNIE. Work, ladies.

WILLIAMINA. I don't know, I kinda like him. He wouldn't be bad to marry.

HENRIETTA. Then *you* marry him.

WILLIAMINA. *(To Annie.)* Oh, he's not my type.

HENRIETTA. Whomever's type he is, I couldn't work if I were married, and that is not an option, so my husband would have to be quite the advanced creature to handle that and I'm not sure our Mr. Shaw fits that bill.

ANNIE. Agreed.

HENRIETTA. *(Lost in her thoughts.)* Although I do admire his persistence. And gait. He has a nice gait.

WILLIAMINA. Meow meow.

ANNIE. *(To Will.)* Would you heel.

HENRIETTA. *(Snapping out of it.)* The point is that, like you, my work is my life. And that's just fine with me. And excuse me for saying this Miss Cannon, but — these Mr. Shaws, they all come around, they need this work, they need *you.* Why don't you demand a faculty position?

ANNIE. Because I don't need a title to do the work.

HENRIETTA. But the boys need your work to keep their titles. And eventually one of us *has* to be a … what was it?

WILLIAMINA. Mighty oak.

HENRIETTA. Mighty oak! You deserve it.

ANNIE. Neither of you are getting a raise and that's final.

HENRIETTA. I don't want a raise.

WILLIAMINA. I do.

HENRIETTA. I want a model. Miss Cannon, if they won't give *you* what you deserve, they're never going to give it to any of us.

ANNIE. What do you want them to give you?

HENRIETTA. A *chance*. To show them what we can do.

ANNIE. Which means what?

HENRIETTA. *(Breath.)* I'm seeing things.

ANNIE. Which *means what?*

HENRIETTA. I'm spotting more and more of the blinking stars, the variables? I'm working on the Small Magellanic Clouds and I'm tracking these stars that pulse.

ANNIE. Cepheid stars?

HENRIETTA. I think so. Some of them blink once a week, some take a month.

ANNIE. The fact that Cepheids pulse is not new.

HENRIETTA. I know. It's the amount of them. The large amount I'm finding.

ANNIE. Actually they're quite rare to find.

HENRIETTA. Not if you're doing it right. *(She looks for approval.)*

ANNIE. Continue.

HENRIETTA. I put together a simple comparative that lets me analyze the plates *quickly*. The *same* star field at different times — and you can see that some of the stars are much brighter. And I'm seeing them in most of the plates. Now if these are true Cepheids, and if there're as many of them as I'm starting to see, it could be a big clue.

ANNIE. To what?

HENRIETTA. I don't know. But it's got to be important.

ANNIE. No it doesn't.

HENRIETTA. But my instincts are telling me that —

ANNIE. Dr. Pickering does not pay for those instincts.

HENRIETTA. He doesn't really pay me at all.

ANNIE. Then do the work you're assigned or don't work. *(Williamina throws a paper ball at Annie. Annie concedes, turns back to Henrietta.)* You may, however, stay *after* hours if you'd like, Miss Leavitt.

HENRIETTA. What.

ANNIE. If you're quiet.

HENRIETTA. *Really? REALLY?!*

ANNIE. Only rule was "quiet."

HENRIETTA. Understood. Thank you. *(She does a little silent cheer. Annie thinks this is stupid and walks past Williamina — who grabs her and kisses her cheek. Annie exits. Williamina too. Margaret appears in a letter. Still annoyed.)*

MARGARET. Henrietta, Daddy was wondering if you'd received the book. Or if you'll come home for Christmas? Write back.

HENRIETTA. *(In a letter light.)* Dear, Margie. Sorry we fought. Here's a book for Michael from his favorite aunt. Could you send sweaters? Love, H. *(Margaret gives up, folds some sweaters during the transition …)*

MARGARET. *(Singing.)*
  For the joy of human love,
  Brother, sister, parent, child …
  Friends on earth and friends above …
  For all gentle thoughts and mild.

  Lord of all to Thee we raise
  This our hymn of grateful praise …

Scene 3

Morning. Henrietta is asleep at her desk. About 1905. Peter and Williamina enter.

PETER. Oh my. Is she — ?
WILLIAMINA. Dusting. *Aren't you Miss Leavitt? (Will pokes Henrietta awake; she grabs her hearing-aid.)*
HENRIETTA. What. Yes. Sorry. Up.
PETER. Miss Leavitt, are you ill?
HENRIETTA. Nope. Just. Here. Hello.
PETER. Is she under an influence?
HENRIETTA. Ha. That would be —
WILLIAMINA. Ridiculous.
HENRIETTA. Delightful, but no.
PETER. You slept here?
HENRIETTA. Nono — very little sleeping. These stars, the Cepheids? The pulsating ones?
PETER. I know what they are.
HENRIETTA. There's a shocking amount in the Magellanic Clouds. I've become quite intimate with the Magellanic Clouds.
PETER. I'll let the boys know we'll need to add a few to the register.
HENRIETTA. Two hundred. *(Pause.)*
PETER. Two — ?
HENRIETTA. Hundred.
PETER. Last — ?
HENRIETTA. Night. Yes.
PETER. Oh. *(Pause.)*
HENRIETTA. So. *(Peter and Henrietta are looking at each other. She breaks.)* Why don't I make a habit of this.
PETER. Why don't you.
HENRIETTA. I'm going to take a nap.
WILLIAMINA. Why don't you. *(Gives a thumbs up. Henrietta smiles, starts to exit.)*
PETER. Very good work, Miss Leavitt. It's really very good.

HENRIETTA. *(Smiles at him.)* Thank you. *(She exits one way, Peter exits another. Annie enters — Williamina preemptively shushes her.)*
ANNIE. Where on earth is she going?
WILLIAMINA. She's taking a nap in the file room. And we'll let her.
ANNIE. She *has* an apartment?
WILLIAMINA. You'll want to hear what she's finding.
ANNIE. Then wake her up. *(Peter reenters, flustered, excited, confused.)*
PETER. *(An announcement.)* There is a lot. Going on. In the world. *(Pause.)*
WILLIAMINA. Uh-huh.
PETER. We are in an age of defiance — I mean defying and upturning it all — all the ideas we held, all the things we knew for certain. Fundamentals even. Distance, light, time —
WILLIAMINA. You read that paper, didn't you.
PETER. You've read it?
ANNIE. Relativity.
PETER. Relativity! It's impossible. Except that it isn't. Time is elastic, space is part of time. It's ridiculous.
WILLIAMINA. Doesn't make it wrong.
PETER. Nonono. The idea that there could be galaxies as big as ours? *Outside* of ours? That the universe is *that* large? No!
ANNIE. The theory seems to suggest it.
PETER. But it makes it all undone, untethered. In the history of human thought there was a steady progression of ideas —
WILLIAMINA. Unless you're Catholic.
PETER. Standing on the shoulders of giants is what I mean.
WILLIAMINA. I dunno, there's a lot of stupid giants.
PETER. But we're *modern.* The modern age — building up, building on top of other stately ideas —
WILLIAMINA. Sensible!
PETER. *Yes.*
WILLIAMINA. *(Totally kidding.)* Physics was about wrapped up!
PETER. *Yes.*
WILLIAMINA. But then that fuzzyheaded man blew up your stately foundation.
PETER. You're not supposed to do that to Isaac Newton. *(Will makes the sound of Einstein blowing up Newton.)* What do we grasp? And how? And until what point when it all shifts anyway?
ANNIE. I'm not sure what you're looking to hear, Mr. Shaw.

PETER. *(Re: Henrietta.)* She found something — *is* finding — uncovering, discovering — and I … don't know what that's like. Which makes me think I'm not very good at this. And things might just be too … strange.

WILLIAMINA. You don't usually talk this much when you come up here.

PETER. I don't? I do. Rounds. I come around.

WILLIAMINA. Oh yes, the life affirming *rounds.*

PETER. I'm just doing my job. Trying to.

WILLIAMINA. And you know why she's got something? Because she's *not just* doing hers. Because she knows she's not getting anything handed to her except the corner of someone else's chance. Because we can't use that apparently hyper-sexed telescope you boys get to, but the mind is sexless and so is the sky — Are you made nervous by how many times I've said the word *sex?*

PETER. Somewhat.

WILLIAMINA. Oh good.

PETER. Just. I admire … what you all do. It's … precision.

ANNIE. Thank you. *(Peter leaves. Henrietta walks in grinning — she heard it all.)*

HENRIETTA. What. Was that?

WILLIAMINA. Wonder meeting competence.

ANNIE. You see why we keep him around.

WILLIAMINA. Is it wrong that I like him a wee bit more because of that? 'Cause I quite enjoyed that little fluster. Speaking of, has he proposed yet?

HENRIETTA. What? *What?*

ANNIE. Williamina.

HENRIETTA. To me? No. What? No.

WILLIAMINA. He always seems like he's going to.

ANNIE. That face he makes.

WILLIAMINA. Pinchy.

HENRIETTA. Pinchy? Who's pinchy? No. We've talked about this. Marry? You're not married. You're not married. Nobody's married. Why is this an issue.

ANNIE. It's not an issue.

WILLIAMINA. Not unless you admit it, prove me right, and live happily ever after.

HENRIETTA. Oh God.

ANNIE. *(To Henrietta.)* Our only power is ignoring her.

WILLIAMINA. I'm not laughing at you. I'm not. Love makes us all look a bit stupid.

ANNIE. Pinchy.

HENRIETTA. *Is pinchy good or bad?*

ANNIE. It's all terribly relative. *(Annie and Will burst into laughter. Henrietta gets up to go.)*

WILLIAMINA. Oh Henrietta. It's just life. Ridiculous and miraculous and often not funny at all. But better when you're laughing. Especially husbands.

ANNIE. She had one.

HENRIETTA. You did?

WILLIAMINA. I did. Abandoned me as soon as we docked in Boston. I was 21, pregnant, poor, and Scottish. So I laughed. Found my way to Dr. Pickering, worked his house as a maid, he brought me here, and here I sit. So I laugh, because that seemed to work. *(Peter enters, stops — All three ladies are staring at him. He tries to understand — starts to say something — decides it's best to just back away slowly … Peter exits. Henrietta keeps staring.)* Time to breathe. *(Henrietta lets out a held breath. Transition …)*

Scene 4

Henrietta is working alone at night, no hearing-aid. Annie enters quietly; Henrietta doesn't notice. Henrietta stops looking down at her pages and cries.

Annie tries to leave but bumps into a desk. Henrietta turns, scrambles for her hearing-aid.

HENRIETTA. Miss Cannon. I'm so sorry.

ANNIE. Nono. I'm sorry.

HENRIETTA. I take it out when I work.

ANNIE. Of course. Carry on. Forgot my gloves.

HENRIETTA. Oh no, I was leaving.

ANNIE. No, I'm leaving. I just came for my hat.

HENRIETTA. Your gloves.

31

ANNIE. My gloves. *(Small pause.)*

HENRIETTA. Please don't think I sit here all night crying.

ANNIE. May I *see* what you sit here all night doing?

HENRIETTA. *(Hands Annie her notebook. Annie reads. Nothing.)* The Cepheids. Of course.

ANNIE. You certainly have a knack for finding them.

HENRIETTA. But I'm finding that *finding* them isn't really worth much if they don't mean anything. And right now they don't.

ANNIE. They might.

HENRIETTA. I'm going on two thousand of them. And I'm starting to think it's like counting grass. You can count it, but why?

ANNIE. I *do* know the feeling. Show me what you've found.

HENRIETTA. *(Showing the ledger. Annie keeps reading. Nothing.)* The left side is a list of Cepheids arranged by fastest period of brightness. The middle column is their spectral class but I think I need to change it to luminosity because I'm not coming up with anything. There's no pattern.

ANNIE. No there's not.

HENRIETTA. I've wasted so much time on this.

ANNIE. Miss Leavitt —

HENRIETTA. I really thought I could sense something in the numbers. Really feel there was something important we weren't connecting, but no —

ANNIE. Miss Leavitt.

HENRIETTA. *Twelve* notebooks packed, staring at me, loose ends all loose and nothing to show and no meaning and nothing, *nothing* makes any damn sense.

ANNIE. Henrietta.

HENRIETTA. Excuse my language.

ANNIE. You're close. Keep working. Think about how you're thinking. It's in there.

HENRIETTA. Should I ask Dr. Pickering?

ANNIE. No.

HENRIETTA. Mr. Shaw.

ANNIE. Oh no. This one's yours.

HENRIETTA. Thank you.

ANNIE. Miss Leavitt, I think you're in the middle of it.

HENRIETTA. Of what?

ANNIE. That chance. *(She pulls out gloves from her coat pocket and puts them on. Annie leaves. Henrietta smiles, breathes. She takes out a spanker and does some kind of celebratory dance thing. Peter enters.)*

HENRIETTA. Oh my God.

PETER. Oh my God. Not to worry.

HENRIETTA. This is just —

PETER. Imposition, so sorry.

HENRIETTA. This is —

PETER. My fault completely.

HENRIETTA. This is *so* exciting! She's right, I push through it, charge through it, matter of time — I know the answer is there — I just keep going. Right? Yes! Hi. *(Lovely awkward pause.)*

PETER. Hello. I just came by for my … hat.

HENRIETTA. Oh.

PETER. My gloves — left my gloves — and I saw the light and I thought, "Well I wonder how all the spanking is going."

HENRIETTA. Might we all agree to another name for that?

PETER. I think that's for the best.

HENRIETTA. Mr. Shaw, I know I shouldn't be here this late.

PETER. Actually I'd prefer it — much prefer it if you called me by my given name. Peter. Would be — nicer, nice.

HENRIETTA. Oh. Henrietta.

PETER. Good. *(Takes his gloves out of his pocket.)* Found them. *(Starts to go but doesn't —)* Miss — Henrietta — I — I don't know anything about you really and — and that's a shame. So. Might I know something about you? Now. Would be nice.

HENRIETTA. Oh. I grew up in Lancaster, family in Wisconsin, my hearing's not great, and I used my dowry to get here, which is why I'm a bit zealous about all this.

PETER. Ah.

HENRIETTA. And I play the clarinet. Not well.

PETER. I play also. Also not well.

HENRIETTA. Then we could be terrible together! I mean — that's not what I mean. I have a habit of blurting.

PETER. And I have a Dachshund. Named Carl. Which is fun. *(He smiles, she smiles. He wants to say … but doesn't.)* Carl awaits. *(Peter leaves, forgetting his hat. Henrietta smiles. Picks up his hat. Flips it and puts it on her head. Peter returns.)* Sorry. Hat. *(Henrietta hands him the hat. He touches her hand.)* I think that … you might be quite … marvelous. I think that. Often. *(Silence. He leaves.)*

HENRIETTA. Oh that is not standard. *(She smiles. Peter enters again. This is an outpouring of pent-up romantic enthusiasm in nearly one breath.)*

PETER. There's an ocean liner leaving tomorrow — You should be on it — I'll be on it — I'm saying come with me — to Europe — For a month — or two? You don't have to decide now — but close to now because the liner leaves tomorrow — I said that — Pack warmly — cold at night — We might stop in Spain — And there's dancing and lobster and water and moonlight and bobbing around and that's romantic — or sickening — Either way there'll be an eclipse. Which is fun.

HENRIETTA. I ... oh my ... yes, that sounds ... very interesting.

PETER. Interesting?

HENRIETTA. Incredible.

PETER. Oh good.

HENRIETTA. If it weren't on a boat.

PETER. You don't like boats? I didn't think of that.

HENRIETTA. No, I just can't leave my work. I'm very close to something and —

PETER. The ladies can't manage?

HENRIETTA. Not *this* work, no. It's my findings and I've worked so hard and —

PETER. You don't have to leave it. I can pack them. You and me *and* work.

HENRIETTA. They crack.

PETER. So they'll be here when we get back.

HENRIETTA. I'm too close to leave — I'm so close.

PETER. But we could meet astronomers all over Europe. Talk about your ideas. See the world!

HENRIETTA. That sounds marvelous but why don't we just go to dinner?

PETER. Because you're always up here!

HENRIETTA. Then I can't go to Europe!

PETER. Henrietta.

HENRIETTA. Peter.

PETER. This is a rather large moment for me so I just want to be clear because it took me three years to get this far. So. Your mind and spirit ... I quite adore ... those things ... about you. And I don't expect you to reciprocate immediately or at all, but I feared combusting if I didn't tell you that you've been the brightest object in my day since we met. And we work with stars. And I know I haven't been the most emotive suitor but I have been a thoughtful one, and I hope that counts for something. And I also hope I do not offend you by expressing how very deeply I ... admire you.

HENRIETTA. Well. I think it's an accurate statement to say that I ... approve.

PETER. You do? That's just tremendous. And a bit shocking, I thought I might have ruined it with that first impression. Or the second. Or this one.

HENRIETTA. Fortune favors the unashamed. But. My work is very important to me and if there is any resistance to that then you might reconsider your adoration promptly.

PETER. I couldn't reconsider if I tried. I know you and I know your work and ... if you can't go with me, I'll stay. Because I cannot walk away from this.

HENRIETTA. What *is* this exactly?

PETER. Well it's — it's love right?

HENRIETTA. I don't know. Is it?

PETER. It's got to be. My heart's beating like a train. That's your fault.

HENRIETTA. *My* fault?! It's *your* fault.

PETER. Yes! See? Love!

HENRIETTA. How, God, *how* do you know that?

PETER. Comparative analysis. Before you: content. After you? Passionate, confident ... idiot. Rounds? Please. An ocean liner? Just to be with you in the widest world. And finally I tell you. And finally you hear. And finally ... (*Eyes connect. Peter takes her hands ... As the Harvard Observatory falls away into ... The deck of an ocean liner — night. Stars ablaze overhead. A band plays somewhere. He spins her into a dance ... Suddenly — Margaret appears in a telegram —)*

MARGARET. Sister — stop. Come home — stop. Father stroke — stop. (*Henrietta stops. The stars go dark. The dream shatters. The Observatory — Peter and Henrietta alone.*)

HENRIETTA. Oh god. Peter, I'm sorry. I have to go.

PETER. Go? Where? What's wrong?

HENRIETTA. My family needs me. My father. Oh god.

PETER. I can help. I can come with you. Whatever you need.

HENRIETTA. My father is sick, my sister's alone.

PETER. I'm coming.

HENRIETTA. You don't need to do that.

PETER. I can help. I want to help.

HENRIETTA. Thank you and I'm sorry but I have to go home and you have to go to dinner in Europe.

PETER. No.

HENRIETTA. Go, Peter.

PETER. No.

HENRIETTA. I don't want you to miss this because of me. So go. And write me. And come back.

PETER. Alright. Yes. But —

HENRIETTA. Go. We go, we come back. And then we ...

PETER. Continue the great experiment of our mutual compatibility.

HENRIETTA. And weather the storm of Williamina's laughter at our expense.

PETER. I imagine it will be thunderous.

HENRIETTA. I'm certain of it.

PETER. So. You leave for a while, and I leave for a while.

HENRIETTA. It's just space.

PETER. And time.

HENRIETTA. Which leaves us...?

PETER. Afar. But not apart.

HENRIETTA. Afar. But not apart. I like that. *(Henrietta kisses him sweetly on the cheek. Then Peter kisses her gorgeously, passionately. Wow. But Peter and the Harvard Observatory are swept away from her as the Leavitt home takes its place.)*

Scene 5

Leavitt home — no stars. Henrietta comes to a stop in front of a waiting Margaret. A box or two of glass star plates sit next to her.

HENRIETTA. Hello. Margie, I'm here.

MARGARET. Henri. Come in. Hello. Come in. Everything's a wreck. Glad you're here.

HENRIETTA. How can I help? What can I do?

MARGARET. Everything. Nothing. It's been a mess since last Sunday.

HENRIETTA. Last Sunday?

MARGARET. We couldn't get ahold of you.

HENRIETTA. I would've come sooner. I didn't know. What happened?

MARGARET. He just fell over. Couldn't talk. Couldn't move.

36

HENRIETTA. Is there anything I can — ?

MARGARET. I don't know where to start. He can't do anything. I'm at my wits' end.

HENRIETTA. Where's Sam?

MARGARET. Trying to organize for Sunday. When the town preacher can't preach — And with Sam hurt, his leg, he fell — it's just so much. It'll be fine. I'll play so at least it'll sound good.

HENRIETTA. They couldn't find someone else to play on Sunday?

MARGARET. *I can play. (Pause.)*

HENRIETTA. I'm so sorry you've had to do this on your own.

MARGARET. Well. There it is. *(Margaret sits. She's exhausted. Sees the boxes of plates.)* What's that?

HENRIETTA. Work. A little.

MARGARET. You don't think this might be the time to put the work down.

HENRIETTA. It's important.

MARGARET. And this is not?

HENRIETTA. No. I mean Yes. I mean I'm here. I'm right here.

MARGARET. I just wonder why you exceed expectation in everything except this family. Even so, Daddy is so proud. You think he isn't. You think he resents your "great escape," and because you never wrote or came home, you wouldn't know. You also wouldn't know that I made you up for him. I wrote letters for you, "from you," brought them in the house every week — So happy — thrilled! — Read them to the whole family — "Look what we got from Henrietta today!" "Oh Daddy, she says hello, she says she loves you, thank you." On and on. Such a comforting fiction.

HENRIETTA. You didn't have to do that.

MARGARET. I did. So that you could have a home to come back to. *(She goes.)*

HENRIETTA. Margie, please —

MARGARET. I am so busy. He'll need to be fed, the doctor's coming in an hour. This is suddenly a lot of work and I am quite sure you'll be leaving any minute so I better not get comfortable.

HENRIETTA. Margie, please stop. *(Touches her. Connects with her.)*

MARGARET. *(Asking what she never asks.)* Please. Help me.

HENRIETTA. I am not leaving. However long you need me. I will not go.

MARGARET. But your work.

HENRIETTA. Is portable. They can send more and I can stay here. I want to. I do. I do. *(Margaret stops. Breath. Then scared, letting it go.)*

MARGARET. It's been so much. Too much.

HENRIETTA. I see that and I'm so sorry.

MARGARET. He was fine and then not and now … Everything changes. Why does *everything* change?

HENRIETTA. *(Tentatively.)* Not changes, just changes form.

MARGARET. What?

HENRIETTA. There's a new theory. A German physicist —

MARGARET. Oh God.

HENRIETTA. Wait, he says that mass and energy are just different forms of the same thing. They shift back and forth forever. So nothing's gone. It just shifts. *(Beat.)* Why don't you practice for Sunday. I'll find Sam, and see if I can help. *(Margaret nods. Goes to her piano. Plays "For the Beauty of the Earth." Annie and Will appear faraway, together looking up. A letter.)* Dear Dr. Pickering, Miss Fleming, Miss Cannon … *(Peter appears faraway, looking at Henrietta.)* Due to family needs, I must remain here. Send more sky. *(Henrietta looks out over us as time passes … Letters … Peter on a ship. Henri at home.)* Dear Peter, I imagine you on the sea, night brilliant with stars. Instead, I spend the nights just as I did as a child — alone in the yard, looking up, dreaming of another life. Yours,

PETER. Dear Henrietta,   HENRIETTA. Henrietta.

Landed in England. Eclipse was stunning. You are … everywhere. Afar but not apart,

HENRIETTA. Peter,   PETER. Peter.

It's hard not to feel like I've gone backwards. But it's good that I'm here. Father's not improving and Margie is so glad to have me. But I do miss … everything.

PETER. Henrietta,   HENRIETTA. Henrietta.

Met the most brilliant men at Oxford, everyone discussing relativity. Paris was great, Zurich was cold. How are things at Harvard?

HENRIETTA. Peter,   PETER. Peter.

I haven't yet returned. But once I help Margie I intend to make my way back to my perfectly creaky desk. And your "rounds."

PETER. Henrietta,   HENRIETTA. Henrietta.

I just arrived in Cambridge and I have so much to tell you. When will you return?

HENRIETTA. Peter,   PETER. Peter.

I promise I'm coming as soon as I can.

PETER. But when will that be? We need you here.

HENRIETTA. Please send more plates.

PETER. I don't care about the plates. Where are you?

HENRIETTA. The same place: Afar but … *(Perhaps she expects him to complete her sentence …)* not apart? *(No response from Peter. An offering.)* Peter? *(No response from Peter.)* Father's funeral was brief but full of friends. Which was good for the family. *(No response from Peter.)* It's been so long since I've heard from you. I fear my letters have gotten lost. Or you have.

PETER. Miss Leavitt,   HENRIETTA. Henrietta.

I am very sorry to hear of your father's passing. *(Different, formal now.)* Harvard's very busy. Dr. Pickering is sending more plates for analysis. If you can manage.

HENRIETTA. Of course I can manage. And I'll be coming back soon.

PETER. *(Not a letter, a crack into his heart, which doesn't know what to say …)* Of course you will. I just wish … *(Lights dim, transition to …)*

Scene 6

Henrietta sits at a table trying to look at the star plates, but there's not enough light, she doesn't have the equipment … Margaret plays …

MARGARET. *(Sings.)*
   For the wonder of each hour
   Of the day and of the night
   Hill and vale and tree and flower
(While working Henrietta sings, almost unconsciously, with Margaret on the last verse …)

MARGARET and HENRIETTA.
   Sun and moon and stars of light …
(Beat. Margaret stops playing, approaches.)

MARGARET. I think it's time we built you a study for all these boxes.

HENRIETTA. I'm sorry.

MARGARET. Or a ranch.

HENRIETTA. I can move them. I know it's a lot. They've been sending more and more. Which is good, I want to work, I *need* to work.
MARGARET. And now that things are calm. You should think about going back. *(Henrietta looks up — thrilled.)* Don't look so excited — I'm not being nice — I just can't stand all these boxes in my house. And Daddy would've wanted you to go.
HENRIETTA. Why are you so good to me?
MARGARET. Because I'm a saint, and you're easy to pity.
HENRIETTA. I accept that. Can I take your son with me — he knows three whole constellations.
MARGARET. Yes, boys and glassware is a good idea. *(Picks up a star plate.)* It amazes me that the entire sky fits on these little window-panes. And how shockingly full it all is. It doesn't look that full from the back yard. But every one of them is just bursting with stars.
HENRIETTA. And nebulae. *(Showing her on a plate.)* There and … there.
MARGARET. My goodness. It's a whole other world up there.
HENRIETTA. Or worlds. You know they call me a *fiend.*
MARGARET. Who calls you a fiend?
HENRIETTA. "A star-finding fiend." One of the most prominent astronomers at Princeton said that about me.
MARGARET. You're important to them?
HENRIETTA. I am actually.
MARGARET. They're not taking advantage of you?
HENRIETTA. Oh they're surely are. But it's a compliment.
MARGARET. A love letter is a compliment.
HENRIETTA. We've talked about this.
MARGARET. Sitting at Harvard and you can't find a gentleman?
HENRIETTA. My department is all women.
MARGARET. Well, get out.
HENRIETTA. It's complicated.
MARGARET. Wouldn't be romance without. Is it?
HENRIETTA. What?
MARGARET. Romance?
HENRIETTA. *No.* Not … yet.
MARGARET. And who is this "not yet"?
HENRIETTA. What about your music?
MARGARET. What about your secret fancy?
HENRIETTA. Margie. It's nothing. It's a boring story with a boring ending.

MARGARET. Why?

HENRIETTA. Because it ended. Or … didn't really start. It's unclear.

MARGARET. I'm sorry.

HENRIETTA. That was never in my plan anyway.

MARGARET. Maybe it's your plan that's boring.

HENRIETTA. Oh just play something would you.

MARGARET. You can't distract me with my own music.

HENRIETTA. It's not a distraction, it's a celebration.

MARGARET. That you're leaving me? Again?

HENRIETTA. I've been hearing bits and pieces for months now. I want to hear the whole of it before I go.

MARGARET. Well. I have been working on something — tiny — just a sketch.

HENRIETTA. A hymn?

MARGARET. Concerto.

HENRIETTA. Really?

MARGARET. I'm working on a symphony.

HENRIETTA. My goodness. I guess I thought — to write a whole symphony I thought you had to be —

MARGARET. Male.

HENRIETTA. European and angry.

MARGARET. Upsetting tradition might just run in the family. *(Pause. Grin. Margaret plays a simple, lovely piece on the piano. Henrietta takes it in. Henrietta notices the stars above her starting to shine again … They appear in time with Margaret's music … Margaret stops playing — the stars stop blinking.)* What's wrong?

HENRIETTA. Keep going — keep — yes, *please play. (Margaret plays — the stars blink to her music Henrietta grabs her logbook — scanning it wildly —)* Oh my God.

MARGARET. What?

HENRIETTA. It's — it's tonal.

MARGARET. It's what? *(Stops playing.)*

HENRIETTA. *Play. (Margaret plays. A letter light on Annie and Will — this is the slight future.)*

WILLIAMINA. Henrietta's written another letter!

ANNIE. That's not a letter, that's a book.

WILLIAMINA. She's found something.

HENRIETTA. It's — the whole thing — it's like music.

MARGARET. My music?

HENRIETTA. The stars are music.

MARGARET. *My* music?

HENRIETTA. The pattern. The numbers — When you put them in the right order — they're — Oh my God the blinking is music — so simple — Right there!

MARGARET. What's right there?! *(The letter.)*

ANNIE. She found a pattern in the Cepheids.

WILLIAMINA. Look at that. The pulsing isn't random —

HENRIETTA. The pulsing isn't random. There *is* a pattern. *(Her big idea.)* The brightest stars take the longest to blink.

ANNIE. It's so simple.

WILLIAMINA. I love it when it's simple.

MARGARET. I don't understand, how does a pattern help?

HENRIETTA. *(While Margaret plays.) A pattern is a standard!* And if we have a standard we can *compare* stars all over the sky. Right now if we see two stars that look equally bright, we can't tell which one is the *brighter star*, and which one is the *closer* star. But the pulsing can tell us which is which. *The pulsing is the answer.*

MARGARET. And somehow musical?

HENRIETTA. Yes. If you think of the notes as the star's brightness. If *this* is the dimmest the star gets — *(Henrietta hits a low note.)* and *this* is the brightest. *(Hits a high note.)* Then the time it takes to get from here — *(Low note, then every note in between until.)* to here — *(High note.)* could tell us *how bright it actually is*, which we could compare to how it *appears*, which could tell us how far away it is, which we could compare to other stars, *(She plays various chromatic scales — some short, some longer.)* which could tell us how far away *they* are, and if we know *that* we can — We can skip star to star across the deepest space until we know … *(Music — Stars — Music!)*

MARGARET. What.

HENRIETTA. Exactly where we are. *(This is the peak of the music. Henrietta looks to the stars, drops her hearing-aid. Margaret sees the stars too. Annie and Will are celebrating back in Boston! And Peter, alone, reading Henri's letter, proud of her. Blackout but for stars.)*

End of Act One

ACT TWO

Scene 1

December 1910. Ocean liner — at night. Henrietta on the deck, looking up at the sky, no hearing-aid. Peter enters next to her.

PETER. Gorgeous night, Miss Leavitt.
HENRIETTA. It really is, isn't it?
PETER. *(Re: the stars.)* Checking on the children?
HENRIETTA. Tucked in but wide awake.
PETER. Tell me more.
HENRIETTA. Are you tempting me with astronomy?
PETER. That is my greatest asset.
HENRIETTA. Then you would remember from school —
PETER. Your cheek, your neck —
HENRIETTA. Pay attention, young man. Stars are classified by their heat —
PETER. Your eyes, my God.
HENRIETTA. And given one of the letters OBAFGKM —
PETER. And how will I ever remember — I wish there was some phrase — perhaps one with an irresistible directive.
HENRIETTA. "Oh Be A Fine Girl, Kiss — " *(He kisses her.)*
PETER. Now I remember.
HENRIETTA. Let's stay here forever.
PETER. Adrift?
HENRIETTA. Afloat.
PETER. In the sea?
HENRIETTA. In the sky. Always the sky. *(Peter strangely shifts into an echo of himself as ... The ocean liner dissolves around them quickly —)*
PETER. Always.
HENRIETTA. Yes.
PETER. The sky.
HENRIETTA. Yes.

PETER. Send more sky. *(Then Peter is gone. Henrietta is alone.)*

HENRIETTA. What? Peter? *(She retrieves her hearing-aid as her dream fades completely into Harvard Observatory. Peter has changed too — cold, formal.)* Peter.

PETER. Yes? Oh. Miss Leavitt. Hello.

HENRIETTA. Hello.

PETER. You're here.

HENRIETTA. I am. Very here.

PETER. Yes. Well. Welcome back. And I'm ... so glad to read about your work. The pattern. It's very good. Work.

HENRIETTA. It took long enough to find, but in the end it's a compliment to all of us.

PETER. It's kind of you to share credit, but I seem to recall *you* working all those nights alone.

HENRIETTA. *(Immediate embarrassment.)* Usually, yes.

PETER. I'm sorry, I should be going. Welcome back. We'll need your next batch soon.

HENRIETTA. Batch of...?

PETER. Those little Cepheids. You're the fiend.

HENRIETTA. Oh. Well yes but —

PETER. Pickering will be glad to have our best computer back in house. Good day.

HENRIETTA. Wait.

PETER. I really can't talk, Miss Leavitt.

HENRIETTA. But I haven't seen the publication yet. And I was hoping to move past computing to real research —

PETER. I'll let you discuss that with Dr. Pickering, excuse me, I have a class.

HENRIETTA. You're teaching? How nice.

PETER. It is a university.

HENRIETTA. Peter.

PETER. Miss Leavitt. *(She steps to him.)* Please don't.

HENRIETTA. Don't what?

PETER. I can't, I'm sorry.

HENRIETTA. I thought we could —

PETER. Miss Leavitt. I cannot talk right now. I'm sorry.

HENRIETTA. I know it's been so long.

PETER. *It has.*

HENRIETTA. I couldn't come back right away, I tried, I did, but there were complications.

PETER. *(Letting it out.)* Years of complications? *(Stuffing it back in.)* I'm sorry. We shouldn't be — I should go.

HENRIETTA. Peter.

PETER. Excuse me.

HENRIETTA. *You* stopped writing to *me.*

PETER. Well. There were complications.

HENRIETTA. And space and time — yes, I know — But when I saw the truth in those numbers, when I finally felt that thing I've always wanted to feel, I thought of you. Because you understand. I thought. *(Peter steps towards her — God, he loves her. Beat — almost speaks — She does too — but then …)*

WILLIAMINA. *(Bursts in, handing her the journal.)* You know, there should be mandatory exclamation points with this sorta thing. I saw you coming up the path and about bit my fist I was so pleased. *(Hugs her hard.)* Hello, darling. Here ya go. *(Reading aloud.)* "'The Period-Luminosity Relation' by Miss Henrietta Leavitt." Blah blah blah — ah! — "There is a simple relation between the brightness of the Cepheid stars and their time periods." Ha! Published and triumphant you stand. *(Pause.)* In case those were worry lines. *(To Peter.)* Why don't you tell her it's brilliant.

PETER. It is an achievement. Especially now that Pickering and the lot have their hands on it.

WILLIAMINA. "The lot" have nothing to do with it.

PETER. I'm saying that when others have a chance to apply it — progress, indeed.

WILLIAMINA. You wouldn't know progress if it swam up and bit your ear.

PETER. Excuse me.

WILLIAMINA. I don't blame you for being jealous —

PETER. I'm not *jealous.*

WILLIAMINA. And *I'm* not standing right in front of you.

HENRIETTA. I'd like to ask Dr. Pickering if I might continue working on this now that I'm back. Perhaps start a project just for the Cepheids —

PETER. We already started one.

HENRIETTA. You what? But I want to participate.

PETER. You're not an astronomer.

HENRIETTA. Of course I am.

PETER. Not without a degree.

HENRIETTA. Then I'll get one.

PETER. And who will do your work?

HENRIETTA. This *is* my work.

PETER. It's not.

HENRIETTA. My work!

PETER. Not any more.

HENRIETTA. *Peter.*

PETER. *Miss Leavitt.* You've done a good job. Let's let that be that.

HENRIETTA. No! The impact of this could — it could change the very —

PETER. *It's just a pattern, Miss Leavitt, it's not a revolution. (Calming down, apologizing.)* Though we, of course, thank you for your contribution. *(Tension. Pause.)*

WILLIAMINA. You are a giant ass.

PETER. I'm sorry I raised my voice

WILLIAMINA. Why don't you GET OUT.

PETER. I will not.

WILLIAMINA. DO NOT PRESS ME.

PETER. After all I've put up with from this department — Where is Miss Cannon? Hm? Gone *again.*

WILLIAMINA. She's sick. Of you.

PETER. We all know where she is — She's out — *Making trouble for this institution.*

WILLIAMINA. And if you ever made as many *contributions* as she makes *trouble* in *one* day? *Any one* of us would care what *you* think about *any one of us.*

PETER. I'll go.

HENRIETTA. Home to your Dachshund?

PETER. To my wife. *(Henrietta drops a glass plate — it cracks. Silence.)* That's ruined. *(Peter starts to go — stops — wants to apologize — doesn't. Exits. Silence. As they clean up the glass plate.)*

WILLIAMINA. Dr. Pickering is finally getting us new chairs.

HENRIETTA. That's ... that's very ...

WILLIAMINA. Darling. We are in the business of perspective. *You* know it's fundamentally hard to tell if something is big and bright or ... just close by.

HENRIETTA. I don't know what you mean.

WILLIAMINA. And if hearts were stars we'd all connect the damned dots.

HENRIETTA. Oh nothing ever ... materialized.

WILLIAMINA. Not saying it did. Just ... Hearts and stars. Can be blinding. *(A moment.)*

HENRIETTA. *(Is she talking about Peter or the Cepheids?)* How do we know that any of this matters? How does anyone know that? I want to know that.

WILLIAMINA. You can't. Which is why you must never doubt or you'll drown. Now. Annie'll be so happy to see you. She's on her way back from a protest. Very exciting these days. And they gave her a sash. She loves that sash. Both of them are off to change the nation. *(Pause. Annie enters.)* Speaking of ... *(To Annie.)* Look who's back, Annie.

ANNIE. Miss Leavitt.

HENRIETTA. Miss Cannon.

ANNIE. Here you are. Welcome.

HENRIETTA. It's so good to see you. *(She hugs Annie. A little much. Annie awkwardly pats her on the back, pries herself off.)*

ANNIE. And you, my dear. The responses to your finding have been numerous.

HENRIETTA. It was in there. You were right.

ANNIE. Then let's all never doubt me again, shall we?

WILLIAMINA. *(To Henri.)* See? *(To Annie.)* How goes the march? I defended your honor.

ANNIE. It was profound and pointless as these things tend to be.

WILLIAMINA. And the sash?

ANNIE. Patriot thread. *(Reveals her suffragette sash — "Votes for Women!")* So you're back for good, I hope. Can we start you on something new then? How do feel about supernovae?

HENRIETTA. Miss Cannon. I'd much rather continue with the Cepheids, keep working with them, follow it through.

ANNIE. Through to where?

HENRIETTA. To some ... true ... *place*.

WILLIAMINA. Put a big red X on it if you find it.

HENRIETTA. *If we're not finding the largest truth then what have we spent our lives doing? What's the point of all this? (The Observatory falls away as Henrietta watches the following in another space ... Peter appears in a spot. He's giving a lecture ...)*

PETER. The cosmic question of our age —

HENRIETTA. What is "the point"?

PETER. What is "the universe"? The question itself admits a singularity of size — We are stuck —

HENRIETTA. We are stuck —

PETER. On this planet.

HENRIETTA. In this life. And our perspective is —

PETER. Our perspective is —

HENRIETTA. Intimate.

PETER. Imperfect.

HENRIETTA. Which means that I might have forgotten —

PETER. However —

HENRIETTA. To live.

PETER. Because we lack the measurements, we are left wondering: How big is everything? Which leads to the central question — Is everything contained within our Milky Way or not?

HENRIETTA. Are we contained or not?

PETER. Is all that we see —

HENRIETTA. Is all that we see —

PETER. The extent of the universe?

HENRIETTA. The extent? No. *No.*

PETER. Absolutely. *(Henrietta is shocked by this. She is now watching his lecture from the back of the room.)* It is my judgment that the universe is exactly the same thing as the Milky Way Galaxy. There is nothing greater and nowhere else. How could there be? To even consider that would mean that these stars are thousands of light years away. And nothing is thousands of light years away. The universe is simply not that vast. Nor need it be to inspire the deepest human wonder. Thank you. *(Henrietta walks right up to Peter.)*

HENRIETTA. Professor Shaw.

PETER. Miss Leavitt. You were watching?

HENRIETTA. How could you say that the universe "isn't that vast." How could you say that?

PETER. Because the majority of astronomers agree.

HENRIETTA. No they don't.

PETER. The ones that matter do.

HENRIETTA. The ones who gave you this job do.

PETER. If you look at the literature —

HENRIETTA. Which I have, Mr. Shaw. Which is where *my finding* is now quite at home.

PETER. Then you'd see, Miss Leavitt, that there is simply no other way to think.

HENRIETTA. Well it's a good thing the universe doesn't care what you think. Or me. Or Newton, or Kepler. It just marches on.

And waits for the blind to catch up. That would be you. *(Starts to leave. Comes back.)* That would be you.

PETER. Henrietta.

HENRIETTA. *I'm sorry but I have to go — I always have to go —*

PETER. Henrietta please.

HENRIETTA. *What. (He stops her, checks to make sure they're alone.)*

PETER. When I came back from Europe my father decided that it was time. And that she was a good match. And I barely knew what happened, and I barely knew her. And I don't know why I acted that way. Yes I do. Seeing you is … Very hard.

HENRIETTA. I am so sorry that this has been so hard. For you.

PETER. That's not what I meant. Perhaps we could talk.

HENRIETTA. We can't.

PETER. Why?

HENRIETTA. Because. There's a boat that leaves tomorrow. For Europe. And I just decided that I'll be on it. Because I've heard that seeing the stars from the sea is not to be missed. And I don't want to miss anything else. And apparently there's lobster.

PETER. That's … that's … good for you. But — wait. I need to say — I should say … that your findings *are* very important and I am *very* proud of … you.

HENRIETTA. Thank you. *(After a moment of looking … A transition sweeps Peter off and sweeps into …)*

Scene 2

Henrietta on that ocean liner at night. She is alone. Noise of people around her though. The sounds of a ship. She is so thoroughly happy. This is real ... not a dream. She looks up. A letter to Margaret ...

MARGARET. "Dear Margie," *(But faraway, Peter reads a letter from Henrietta as well.)*

PETER. "Dear Mr. Shaw,"

HENRIETTA. I would like to say that I wish I could send you an image of this sky tonight. But I hope we never invent pictures that perfect — that would miss the point.

PETER. "'Which is what?' I think staring out to sea."

HENRIETTA. I used to think that to *be truly alive* I needed answers. I needed to *know*. But all this does not in fact *need* to be known, does it? *We* do.

PETER. "*We* do."

HENRIETTA. Because the real point ... is seeing something bigger. And knowing we're a small part of it, if we're lucky. In the end that is a life well-lived.

PETER. "Please tell Miss Cannon that when I come back ... I have work to do."

HENRIETTA. Because thank God there's a lot out there bigger than me. See you soon. *(Peter and the ocean liner fade into time and distance ... as Henrietta returns home on a huge ship greeted by Margaret with a huge wave ...)*

MARGARET. Henrietta!   HENRIETTA. Henrietta.
(The sisters hug a long hug.)

HENRIETTA. Margie! I missed you so much. Welcome to Boston.

MARGARET. And the same to you. Welcome back. Now tell me everything.

HENRIETTA. Well Paris *is* as perfect as you'd like to think and London is just — *(Henrietta staggers, sits, then cringes as a pain sweeps over her abdomen.)*

MARGARET. Henri. *Henri.*

HENRIETTA. I'm fine.

MARGARET. You're not fine. What is this?

HENRIETTA. It's nothing. It passes.

MARGARET. It's not nothing. You should have come home *immediately*.

HENRIETTA. There were only a few bad days.

MARGARET. Henrietta, they've invented doctors.

HENRIETTA. I saw one in London.

MARGARET. And you're seeing another one right now.

HENRIETTA. Margie, no —

MARGARET. The luggage can wait.

HENRIETTA. I'm going straight to Harvard —

MARGARET. You're coming back to Wisconsin with me — you're resting and —

HENRIETTA. I'm going to work — I want to work —

MARGARET. I don't care. There's time for all that —

HENRIETTA. *There's not. (Pause. Her look tells Margie it's serious.)*

WILLIAMINA. Wait now, there she is! Henri!

ANNIE. Henrietta! There she is.

WILLIAMINA. That's what I said. I said that was her. Henrietta, dear!

HENRIETTA. Oh my goodness, what are you doing here?

ANNIE. What are we doing here? Your sister told us you were finally coming back.

WILLIAMINA. And you have to save us from each other.

ANNIE. You really do. Now, we have a mountain of work to get through.

WILLIAMINA. *(To Margaret.)* Hello, you, I'm Williamina.

MARGARET. I'm Margaret. Hello.

HENRIETTA. Oh, this is my sister Margie. I thought you'd met.

MARGARET. Not yet, but I've heard so much — *(Annie gives Margaret an uncharacteristically large hug.)*

ANNIE. You're the sister! We've heard of you!

MARGARET. Oh my.

WILLIAMINA. You're scaring the poor thing, Annie.

ANNIE. Unfortunately common.

WILLIAMINA. Didn't Henrietta say you have a son?

MARGARET. I do. As tall as his father, and twice the charmer.

WILLIAMINA. Oh dear.

MARGARET. Let's just say that I do not fear a lack of grandchildren.

WILLIAMINA. Send him to me, I'll straighten him out.

ANNIE. Alright, ladies. The early graphs from Princeton are in and we need your eyes on them.

HENRIETTA. I can do that.

MARGARET. Henri, wait — *(To Annie.)* She was just saying she's been a bit poorly these days.

HENRIETTA. I'm fine and I'm so looking forward to being back.

ANNIE. You're sick?

HENRIETTA. No.

MARGARET. *Yes.* She nearly fainted just now — She's not well — and I really must insist —

HENRIETTA. *I'm* insisting, Margie. My work is here. And my life, and every chance I've ever had. Is here. *(Pause.)*

MARGARET. Then so am I. You can't get rid of me.

WILLIAMINA. Me neither.

ANNIE. And you can work from home when you like, so there's not a single reason we can't all go about our business as usual.

HENRIETTA. Thank you. Lunatic women. *(She braves a small pain again. She leans on Margie.)*

WILLIAMINA. *(Helping her ...)* Here we go, darlin'.

ANNIE. I'll get the bags.

MARGARET. We've got you, Henri. We're right here. *(Helping Henrietta walk off. Transition ...)*

Scene 3

Annie is in the office gathering plates. Peter enters.

PETER. Excuse me. Miss Cannon.

ANNIE. Not today, Mr. Shaw.

PETER. I heard about Henrietta — Miss Leavitt. I heard she's sick? How sick? How is she?

ANNIE. Well she's making do. Working from home just down the street. I think you know that nothing is going to keep her down for long.

PETER. Nothing short of an earthquake.

ANNIE. That sounds about right. *(Pause.)*

PETER. *(Handing her a letter.)* Would you please give her this? I took the liberty of inquiring to a family physician and he said he'd

52

be happy to see her. She would never ask, but ... If you would tell her to please accept his services as a favor to me.

ANNIE. *(The first time they've ever really connected.)* I will. Thank you, Mr. Shaw. That's very ... Thank you. *(She takes his hand, shakes it. They are equals, for a moment at least. Transition to ...)*

Scene 4

Years later. Around 1918. Henrietta is at her small home in Cambridge with Margaret. She sits in a chair, covered by a blanket.

MARGARET. We got the census today. I started to fill it out but I didn't know what to put under your profession?

HENRIETTA. Astronomer is my profession.

MARGARET. Alright.

HENRIETTA. *Astronomer.*

MARGARET. With a capital "A." And how are we doing today?

HENRIETTA. You know the worst part of this? Sitting still.

MARGARET. For you, I'm sure it is. How's the pain?

HENRIETTA. Not bad today.

MARGARET. But relaxing bothers you?

HENRIETTA. You can't order someone to relax and have it be relaxing.

MARGARET. Would you like to read some news?

HENRIETTA. I can't take any more war news. Did they send another astronomy circular?

MARGARET. You'd think a world war would make the stars seem trivial.

HENRIETTA. You'd think stars would make war seem trivial. I have never felt so helpless.

MARGARET. You're not helpless.

HENRIETTA. I write all these letters and no one answers. These men, colleagues, all using my work, but they won't let me near it. Useless. Helpless.

MARGARET. You're getting upset.

HENRIETTA. *Life* is about getting appropriately upset. And all I want to know is what's true — what *else* is true. And how long is

53

that list. And I know I won't know. And what does all the knowing of the not knowing do to a sane person? What does *that* mean?

MARGARET. It could mean that we're all helpless. And alone. And because you can't connect everything yourself that nothing's connected. Or. It could mean that you may not know how you might matter to people right now, and you cannot know how you will matter in the future. But you are *already* connected — and you *already* matter. Because what you do outlasts you. Sometimes. Am I helping or hurting?

HENRIETTA. I can't tell. But thank you. And … I want to explain.

MARGARET. Oh, you've tried explaining it and I'm just too thick.

HENRIETTA. Not stars. Something like … souls.

MARGARET. Henri …

HENRIETTA. I just know that you worry about those things. And I don't want you to think that I don't believe in anything. I do, just a different kind of … Faith in … Grand Observation.

MARGARET. Which is comforting?

HENRIETTA. Which is … nimble. And that is comforting. *My* heaven? Is a cosmos deep in a gorgeous void.

MARGARET. A void?

HENRIETTA. Full darkness —

MARGARET. Not *all* darkness —

HENRIETTA. Mottled with immaculate combustion —

MARGARET. But the stars are —

HENRIETTA. Hot gas in a lonely —

MARGARET. Not lonely —

HENRIETTA. Broad, airless —

MARGARET. Don't say airless —

HENRIETTA. Deep, vast, dark —

MARGARET. Stop it just *StopIt*. Alright. I know we don't speak plainly about this but … Where does *my* heaven go?

HENRIETTA. Maybe it doesn't.

MARGARET. Henri.

HENRIETTA. I'm going first, I'll tell you who's right. *(Pause. Tense. Margaret leaves. Comes back.)*

MARGARET. You cannot say that. Not to me.

HENRIETTA. I've made peace with that part.

MARGARET. I haven't. And what other part is there?

HENRIETTA. The part of meaning something.

MARGARET. You mean everything to me.

54

HENRIETTA. But you have your babies, your music, you … like church.

MARGARET. You can't compare us.

HENRIETTA. You have a life.

MARGARET. And you have a legacy.

HENRIETTA. Work that I can't finish!

MARGARET. That's what a legacy *is*. The way I see it, and this is just how I see it. You asked God a question and He answered. That's the meaning of meaning for most of us. *(Doorbell.)* Now. *Relax before I drug you. (Margaret leaves. Henrietta sits a moment. Margaret returns.)* How about some mail?

HENRIETTA. Fine. *(Margaret reveals — Annie and Williamina. Annie wears pants — which Margaret notices.)*

MARGARET. And messengers.

ANNIE. Henrietta.

WILLIAMINA. Darling.

ANNIE. Margaret dear! Thank you again for keeping Henri so comfortable and close by. To have her just blocks away with all these new girls and their temperaments and their outfits —

MARGARET. *(Looking at those pants.)* Uh-huh.

ANNIE. You would not believe their shoes.

MARGARET. Probably not.

WILLIAMINA. How are you feeling today?

HENRIETTA. Fine. Bored. Angry.

WILLIAMINA. Not for long you're not.

MARGARET. Alright, you ladies chat. I've got dinner for us. You'll both stay. I insist.

WILLIAMINA. Wait now, you should hear this.

HENRIETTA. Hear what?

ANNIE. We have news.

WILLIAMINA. Great news.

HENRIETTA. What news, Annie, *tell me.*

ANNIE. Head of Stellar Photometry. It's yours. Pickering sent me to make the offer.

HENRIETTA. Oh my goodness.

MARGARET. Henri!

ANNIE. And a raise.

WILLIAMINA. Of a quarter.

HENRIETTA. *(To Annie.)* Head of Photometry? But that's *your* job.

ANNIE. Now I'm Head Curator. Everyone's moving up.

WILLIAMINA. Like mighty oaks!

MARGARET. Oh that's wonderful. Congratulations.

ANNIE. It's a great honor, Henrietta.

WILLIAMINA. Like magma from the depths of men's minds, a nice hot compliment erupts.

ANNIE. A change in the system is what it is. A model. For the future.

WILLIAMINA. Oh Lord.

ANNIE. And if we use things like this and take a *real* stand —

WILLIAMINA. She's about to give you a pamphlet.

ANNIE. We can make a larger difference. *(Handing them pamphlets.)*

HENRIETTA. What's all this?

ANNIE. We need a vote, girls. It's about equality —

and it's about time!   WILLIAMINA. "And it's about time!"

WILLIAMINA. I know all the slogans.

MARGARET. Oh. I'm not really —

ANNIE. If we can organize the sky, we can organize our minds to choose our own future.

WILLIAMINA. She heard a speech a year ago and —

ANNIE. Is this a democracy or not?

WILLIAMINA. Now she's a patriot.

ANNIE. A *true* patriot, yes I am. Does it say "We the People" or doesn't it?

WILLIAMINA. It does.

ANNIE. It does! And we're marching in D.C. next month. You should join us. Both of you. *(Pause.)*

MARGARET. I'll read the pamphlet.

WILLIAMINA. It's a great pamphlet.

MARGARET. Glazed ham for dinner. I should get it ready.

HENRIETTA. Thank you, Margie.

WILLIAMINA. Why don't I come and get in the way. *(Margaret and Williamina exit.)*

ANNIE. So. We have new computers. You should come by the office.

HENRIETTA. Trust me, how much I wish I could.

ANNIE. What can I do?

HENRIETTA. I need more work — anyone's, whoever's working on this. I've been keeping up with the circulars. I've been writing everyone I can think of. I need to know what they're seeing. If I can't do the work myself — even the tiniest pinch of information — I'm fine with being tiny — I just need to know.

ANNIE. Of course you do. I'll have some girls take time and investigate.

HENRIETTA. Thank you. All I have is time and all I haven't is time.

ANNIE. Time is … persistent.

HENRIETTA. Yes.

ANNIE. But light, its speed, is a constant — one of the few in the universe. Just so you know. I choose to measure you in light. *(Pause. She grabs Henrietta's hand. Pause.)*

WILLIAMINA. *(Offstage.) Annie.* Ham needs your help.

ANNIE. What on earth? I'll go get your sister. *(Exits. Henrietta reaches for a star plate. Can't get to it without too much pain. Peter enters — out of breath — thrilled, overjoyed, we've haven't seen him like this since his ocean liner proposal.)*

PETER. Miss Leavitt — Hello —

HENRIETTA. Mr. Shaw?

PETER. I'mHere — Iknow — It's odd — but I had to see you.

HENRIETTA. *Why? What's going on?*

PETER. *There's a new finding.* And I don't think I'm overstating — it changes everything. And you had to be the first to know —

HENRIETTA. Mr. Shaw, please tell me what you're talking about, and why you're here, and be aware that they're likely pressed ear-to-grain against that door.

PETER. Well. I didn't know exactly where you lived so it starts with me following them.

WILLIAMINA. *(Offstage.) He followed us? I will smack his — (A scuffle behind the door as Will is dragged away.)*

PETER. That doesn't matter. What matters is that today I received a — well, *you* received, but it all comes to my office now —

HENRIETTA. What comes?

PETER. Letters from colleagues to you.

HENRIETTA. To me?

PETER. I thought they were copied.

HENRIETTA. *They weren't.* I live blocks away! I've been trying to find out what's going on for ages!

PETER. Sorry.

HENRIETTA. Ages!

PETER. The point is. This morning, Hertzsprung — The Danish one?

HENRIETTA. Big beard.

PETER. Right. He used your work to measure the distance to those Cepheids. *(Pause.)*

HENRIETTA. *My* Cepheids?

PETER. In the Small Magellanic Cloud, yes.

HENRIETTA. He calibrated … *actual* distance to my Cepheids?
PETER. This could be the first measurement of anything outside our galaxy.
HENRIETTA. Which means there *are things* outside of our galaxy.
PETER. *(Showing her the letter.) Yes.* Proof. That the universe *is* vast.
HENRIETTA. How did he do it?
PETER. He used statistical parallax for the zero-point against the sun, then plugged in *your* data for the slope and … there you have it.
HENRIETTA. That makes it sound so easy.
PETER. But without your work it was impossible. Your work made the leap — for us all. Now we have a standard measurement — for the rest of time we have a standard. Oh. And another man keeps writing. Hudgins?
HENRIETTA. Hudgins. Hubble?
PETER. *(A ha!) Hubble.* Yes.
HENRIETTA. Peter. How far away are my stars?
PETER. Thousands and thousands of light years away.
HENRIETTA. Oh my God.
PETER. Incredible.
HENRIETTA. Which means our galaxy *could be* one of many.
PETER. Perhaps one of many … billions. *(Beat. Thrilled.)*
HENRIETTA. I knew it.
PETER. You did.
HENRIETTA. You were perfectly wrong.
PETER. I was. Ha! *(Pause. Turning to her, a different energy. This is his version of "I have always loved you.")* I am so proud to know you. *(Handing her a wrapped package.)* And. This was under your desk. A new girl found it. I thought you'd like it back.
HENRIETTA. This. Is the book my father sent me.
PETER. You never opened it?
HENRIETTA. I was too busy. And then too … ashamed, I think. *(Henrietta opens it — it's a book.)* Collected poems.
PETER. Really? *(She shares it with him.)* Whitman.
HENRIETTA. My father sent me poems?
PETER. This one's marked. *(Margaret enters, unseen.)*
    "When I heard the learn'd astronomer,
        When the proofs, the figures, were ranged in columns before
            me,
        When I was shown the charts and the diagrams, to add,
            divide, and measure them,

58

When I sitting heard the astronomer where he lectured with
    much applause in the lecture-room,
How soon, unaccountable, I became tired and sick,
Till rising and gliding out I wander'd off by myself,
In the mystical moist night-air, and from time to time,
Look'd up in perfect silence at the stars."
(Beat.)
MARGARET. So he's not a marauder, then? Williamina had me
worried.
HENRIETTA. Margie, this is Mr. Peter Shaw.
MARGARET. *The* Peter Shaw?
PETER. A pleasure to meet you.
MARGARET. You'll stay for dinner?
PETER. Oh no, I shouldn't —
MARGARET. And yet you will. We have much to discuss, Famous
Mr. Shaw.
HENRIETTA. And Margie is a wonderful musician. Maybe you
and Annie can sing for us.
MARGARET. Oh yes!
PETER. Oh God.
HENRIETTA. Margie knows musicals.
PETER. I couldn't.
HENRIETTA. You're singing.
MARGARET. How nice!
PETER. I've learned just not to argue with women.
MARGARET. That's correct. Dinner is on the table. We'll be there
in just a moment.
HENRIETTA. And you must tell Will and Annie immediately.
MARGARET. About what?
PETER. Henrietta just became the first person to measure the
universe. *(He smiles and exits. Beat.)*
HENRIETTA. You knew about him.
MARGARET. I did.
HENRIETTA. You knew about him the whole time.
MARGARET. I did. That many letters? *(Pause.)*
HENRIETTA. Sisters are strange friends. *(Margaret smiles. Henrietta
takes her hand. Beat. Annie bursts in, followed by Peter and Will, reading
the letter from Hertzsprung.)*
ANNIE. WHAT DID HE JUST TELL ME?
PETER. It's real. I couldn't believe it.

WILLIAMINA. Of course he couldn't.

PETER. *Would you be nice to me?*

ANNIE. Henrietta was right!

WILLIAMINA. You were right! Look at this.

ANNIE. Oh my goodness, look at this!

WILLIAMINA. That's what I said! Look at this! The whole world should be looking at this!

ANNIE. Henrietta.

HENRIETTA. I know.

ANNIE. This is ... This is just ...

WILLIAMINA. It's everything.

ANNIE. It is. Everything. *(A moment for the size of this discovery to sink in ... Annie whispers something to Will.)*

MARGARET. How do you celebrate measuring the universe?

PETER. I have no idea.

MARGARET. I have cookies?

WILLIAMINA. *(To Annie.)* That's brilliant. *(To Henri.)* Alright. Come on. We're celebrating. *(Whispers something to Peter.)*

HENRIETTA. We already are celebrating.

ANNIE. Not enough. And you deserve it.

HENRIETTA. Thank you all but —

PETER. *(To Will.)* That's perfect! Let's do it. Let's do it right now.

HENRIETTA. Do what right now?

MARGARET. What are we doing?

ANNIE. *(To Margaret.)* You're coming too.

MARGARET. Me what? Wait.

HENRIETTA. No. I can't go anywhere.

MARGARET. She's really not supposed to.

PETER. You have to.

ANNIE. You deserve this, Henrietta.

HENRIETTA. It doesn't matter if I can't. *(Annie whispers the plan to Margaret aside ...)*

WILLIAMINA. It's not that far.

PETER. Only a few blocks away.

WILLIAMINA. Just up the hill!

HENRIETTA. It's freezing! I *can't*. Cannot. Go anywhere. So thank you. But let's just sit down, have a nice dinner — *(Margaret gets it, springs into action.)*

MARGARET. Leave the ham, get the car.

HENRIETTA. For a few blocks?

WILLIAMINA. Now we're talking!
HENRIETTA. *Margie.*
MARGARET. Henri. Relax. *(The room falls away as they run off.*
Perhaps Annie and Peter sing into ——)

Scene 5

BOOM. Faraway we hear "For the Beauty of the Earth."

HENRIETTA. *(To us.)* On top of a hill ... Just blocks away ...
Across the courtyard from my old desk ... where it stood off-
limits ... I see. The Great Refractor Telescope. To which we happily
break in that night. And taking Margie's hand. I lean close. Hold
my breath. And see ... *(She gasps.)* My heaven. *(BOOM. Stars*
everywhere — more than ever — Peter, Will, Annie, and Margie fade
as Henrietta takes out her hearing-aid. Tosses it.) Some time from
now I gather myself. And sneak outside — and look up. In perfect
silence. And I know — that distance is only space and time, and for
some of us ... light. I am out of time. But light has never let me
down. And so. I shift. *(She points up. The ocean liner takes over —*
Henrietta stands tall on the deck, breathes deep.) The next year ...
Annie gets a vote. *(Faraway. Annie and Williamina put ballots in a*
box.) The next year, a man named Hubble uses my work to prove that
our most unique galaxy is in fact one of billions ... upon billions.
(Faraway, Peter hears this — wow.) Then a man from Sweden calls
wondering if I might like ... a Nobel Prize. It's too late for me, but
I take the compliment. *(Faraway Annie, Will, Peter, Margaret look*
up.) Another few years and Will dies in Boston, Annie by her side.
(Williamina joins Henrietta on the ocean liner.) Another year and
another war takes over the world. Then Annie dies. *(Annie joins*
Henrietta and Will on the ocean liner.) Then Peter. *(Peter joins them.)*
Then my sister, kissed by twelve grandchildren, a symphony on the
radio. *(Her symphony crackles through a radio as Margaret joins them*
on the ocean liner.) Then we harness the atom, then orbit the Earth,
then stand on the moon. *(Shocking human achievements.)* Then a
telescope named Hubble, with wings set for space, shows us how vast

and beautiful it all is … *(Pictures from Hubble Telescope projected everywhere. The music stops. Silence. True sound of space. The stars begin to take over — the ship, the women, the audience. Spots of light powdering every surface.)* Because wonder will always get us there … Those of us who insist that there is much more beyond ourselves. And I do. *(A pulsing light surrounds and becomes Henrietta. She is now a blinking star.)* And there's a reason we measure it all in light. *(Blackout — but for stars everywhere.)*

End of Play

PROPERTY LIST

Hearing-aid
Star plates in boxes
Star spanker
Notebooks and pencils
Letters
Gloves (man's and woman's)
Man's hat
Piano
Suffragette sash and pamphlet
Luggage
Book of collected poems by Walt Whitman

SOUND EFFECTS

Single musical notes for stars
Romantic far-off music
Doorbell (early 1900s)

Note on Songs/Recordings, Images, or Other Production Design Elements

Be advised that Broadway Licensing neither holds the rights to nor grants permission to use any songs, recordings, images, or other design elements mentioned in the play. It is the responsibility of the producing theater/organization to obtain permission of the copyright owner(s) for any such use. Additional royalty fees may apply for the right to use copyrighted materials.

For any songs/recordings, images, or other design elements mentioned in the play, works in the public domain may be substituted. It is the producing theater/organization's responsibility to ensure the substituted work is indeed in the public domain. Broadway Licensing cannot advise as to whether or not a song/arrangement/recording, image, or other design element is in the public domain.